GOLD! GOLD FROM
THE AMERICAN RIVER!

THE DAY THE GOLD RUSH BEGAN

 Actual Times

VOLUME THREE JANUARY 24, 1848 $8.99

GOLD! GOLD FROM THE AMERICAN RIVER!

BY DON BROWN

SQUARE
FISH

ROARING BROOK PRESS
New York

For Rita-Rita, my own treasure

SQUARE
FISH

An Imprint of Macmillan
175 Fifth Avenue
New York, NY 10010
mackids.com

Square Fish books may be purchased for business or promotional use. For information on bulk purchases,
please contact the Macmillan Corporate and Premium Sales Department at
(800) 221-7945 x 5442 or by e-mail at specialmarkets@macmillan.com.

Library of Congress Cataloging-in-Publication Data
Brown, Don, 1949–
    Gold! Gold from the American River! / Don Brown.
        p. cm.
    ISBN 978-1-250-04060-2 (paperback) / ISBN 978-1-4299-9096-7 (e-book)
    1. California—Gold discoveries—Juvenile literature. 2. California—History—1846–1850—
Juvenile literature. 3. Frontier and pioneer life—California—Juvenile literature. I. Title.
F865.B887 2011   979.4'04—dc22   2010014375

Originally published in the United States by Roaring Brook Press
First Square Fish Edition: 2014
Book designed by Jennifer Browne
Square Fish logo designed by Filomena Tuosto

1 3 5 7 9 10 8 6 4 2

AR: 6.0 / LEXILE: 1010L

January 24, 1848

James Marshall hammered a shiny pebble
beneath a cold, clear January sky.

He'd found the pebble, and another like it, in the runoff ditch of a water-powered sawmill. Marshall and his helpers had built the mill on the American River, one of the many streams and rivers spilling down California's Sierra Nevada mountains.

As Marshall inspected the nearly completed mill, he'd spied the shiny pebbles. He wasn't certain what they were, but he remembered a simple test.

"Putting one of the pieces on a hard river stone, I took another and commenced hammering it. It was soft and didn't break," Marshall said.

To Marshall, soft, shiny stones meant only one thing. Quickly searching out his workers, he exclaimed, "Boys, I believe I found a gold mine!"

His cry would find its way to every corner of the globe.

John Sutter owned the sawmill where Marshall found gold. He needed lumber to erect the personal kingdom he dreamed of establishing in California. New Switzerland, he meant to call it. Sutter, who liked to be called "Captain," had already constructed a fort.

When Marshall announced his discovery, he told only Sutter and people connected to the sawmill.

Then Sam Brannan found out about it. He was a newcomer to Yerba Buena, the tiny Pacific seaport not far from Sutter's mill that would soon change its name to San Francisco.

Brannan decided that wider knowledge of the discovery would attract more gold seekers. And more people meant more opportunities for ambitious businessmen like himself.

With gold dust in hand, he ran through the streets yelling, "Gold! Gold! Gold from the American River!"

The exciting news sent hundreds of people racing to the goldfields. Within weeks the town nearly emptied and San Francisco's population dropped to twelve.

By summer, about four thousand people joined the search for gold.

And, by the ounce, by the pound, some people were finding it.

"Excited rumors began to spread with the rapidity of a great epidemic. To all appearances men seemed to have gone insane," one observer wrote.

Seizing the chance to profit from the madness, Sam Brannan bought twenty-cent pans needed for mining and sold them for as much as sixteen dollars.

Meanwhile, Americans in the East heard rumors of the discovery. Government messengers brought President James Polk samples of California's treasure. On December 5, 1848, he gave a speech declaring that it had an "abundance of gold." Twenty-two million Americans heard the news and came down with a terrific case of gold fever.

By January 1849, thousands of people abandoned their families and jobs and headed for California. They'd be remembered as the forty-niners, in recognition of the great rush that started that year.

Most of the forty-niners lived closer to the Atlantic Coast than they did to the goldfields on the Pacific Coast. The land between the two was an uncharted mystery. No road or railroad connected one coast to the other.

How, then, to get to California?

The forty-niners had three choices. One way was to sail more than thirteen thousand miles from the Atlantic Coast, around the bottom tip of South America, and then to California.

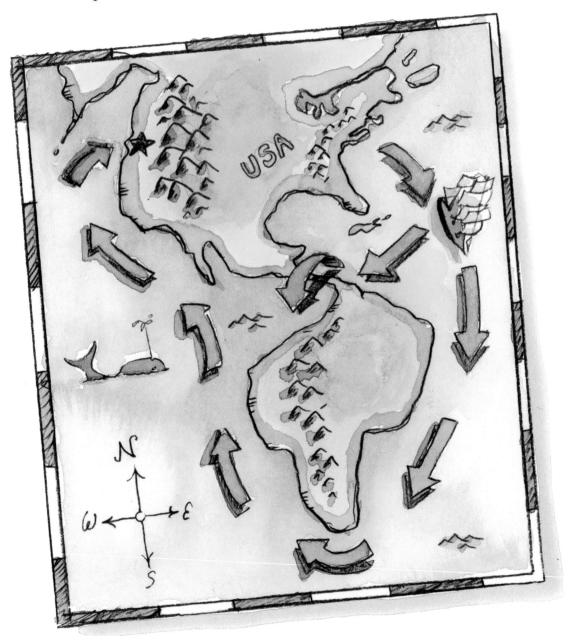

A typical journey would take four to six months; one feeble tub, the *Harford*, took nearly a year. Boredom, seasickness, bad food, and foul water came with every trip . . . as did impossibly cramped decks and quarters.

"Four young men, finding no room for a table to play cards . . . used a [stout man's] stomach for a card table," one traveler said.

Gold seekers could follow a second path and shorten the sea journey by landing on the Atlantic side of the narrow Isthmus of Panama. They then trekked cross-country to the Pacific Ocean. There, another ship would take them to San Francisco . . . if they could find space.

Forty-niner Daniel Knower arrived on the Pacific Coast after a harrowing jungle tramp across the Isthmus and discovered a thousand others competing for sixty berths aboard a single steamer making the California run. Knower's entire journey to California took months.

Most gold rushers took the third and most direct path:
over land, across the continent. In 1849 alone, 22,500 gold
seekers took this route.

With wagons painted with "Wild Yank," "Rough and Ready," "Gold Hunter," or some other inspiring name, they assembled in groups or companies at places like St. Joseph, Missouri, and Council Bluffs, Iowa, on the Missouri River. From there, it was 2,100 miles on the California Trail to the great fortune they were sure awaited them.

The forty-niners pushed off in May as the prairie grass started growing. The new grass would provide feed for the tens of thousands of horses, mules, and oxen dragging the wagons. Then, they traveled for four to five months at sixteen miles a day, day after day, without fail, disregarding sickness, injury, or breakdown. Failing to keep the pace meant the travelers might not make it to the gold fields before winter, leaving them stranded on a snowy, mountainous trail.

But the hazards didn't dampen the forty-niners' enthusiasm. They'd abandoned or postponed their old lives as farmers, dentists, clerks, landlords, shopkeepers, and meant to make the best of the decision. Brimming with supplies and optimism, their eyes fixed on the horizon, they started west . . . and immediately hit a traffic jam.

Hundreds of wagons had to wait their turn to be ferried across the Missouri River, which was something of the border for settled America. "As soon as one wagon enters the boat, the next moves down to the edge of the bank. . . . This goes on from the earliest dawn till midnight, day after day," remarked one forty-niner.

Eventually they joined the snaking line of wagons
that at times seemed endless. One traveler noted, "For
the whole distance in view . . . before and behind us, long
trains were in motion or encamped on the grassy bottom."

Overloaded wagons slowed travel and taxed draft animals. Supplies not essential for the trek were soon tossed aside. Another traveler noted, "We saw castaway articles strewn by the roadside one after another in increasing profusion."

As the forty-niners crossed the plains, spring changed to summer, and then fall. The weather could be unforgiving and cruel. In rain, the trail turned to mud, sticking the wagons fast in the deep muck.

Parching winds and stifling dust blistered lips. Sleet robbed drivers of feeling in their fingers, making it nearly impossible to hold the reins.

The chance for accidents and mishaps during the tough travel was always there, but it was disease, especially cholera, that proved the deadliest risk and greatest killer. One observer counted four fresh graves every day for 170 miles. How many died from disease? Some people say a thousand, others say four thousand.

Although some people gave up and went home, most others doggedly kept up the two-miles-an-hour march. They crossed the plains and reached the Rocky Mountains, something of a halfway mark. Still, a thousand miles remained, including a wasteland known as the Forty Mile Desert.

"Expect to find the worst desert you ever saw, and then find it worse than you expected," advised one veteran of the wasteland.

Another observed, "[It was] the most dreary desolate place. . . . The mules were so hungry they ate dust and gravel. . . . All along the desert road . . . was strewed the dead bodies of oxen, mules, and horses & the stench was horrible."

The path then climbed the Sierra mountains. Travelers arriving before winter counted themselves fortunate. But even snow-free trails wrecked wagons and sent mules pitching off cliffs.

The forty-niners who made it this far were close now. Traveling through slots in the heights called passes, they finally reached Sacramento, the town closest to the goldfields. It had sprung up after the discovery of gold.

By the end of 1849, about sixty-five thousand gold seekers had flooded California, exploding its population by 500 percent. San Francisco, the ocean gateway to the goldfields, swelled from as few as twelve people to about five thousand.

Beside the crowded town, ships choked the San Francisco harbor. "I saw about 500 vessels. . . . Some were rotting. . . . The sailors had all ran off to the mines," said new arrival Sam McNeil.

The newcomers erected canvas houses. At night, lamplight seemed to transform them to dwellings of solid light.

The sailors were but a few of the thousands pouring into the mountains. Crude mining camps sprang up everywhere. The makeshift towns took names like Rat Trap Slide, Chucklehead Diggings, Jackass Gulch, Shinbone Peak, and Quack Hill. "Sometimes they're tents, sometimes they're buildings, sometimes they're just a table under a tree," said one forty-niner. Scattered about the camps was the trash from countless miners: "empty tins of preserved meats, sardines, and oysters, empty bottles of all shapes and sizes, innumerable ham-bones, old clothes, and other rubbish."

All of the forty-niners saw treasure in their futures, but their first discovery was of expensive supplies.

"I paid sixteen dollars for a shovel, eight dollars for a pick, four for a gold pan, and thirty-two dollars for a pair of boots," remembered one miner of his first experience.

The forty-niners and their high-priced equipment joined the goldfields or "diggings."

"That was the word, the diggings . . . because that's what [miners] were doing," explained one man. "There [were] river banks, river bars, dried creeks, rocks, rocks, by the millions, and the gold [was] beneath those rocks. . . . You're working in freezing water up to your waist for hours at a time. You're reaching down, moving rocks, bringing in the rock and the gravel and working it all the time, with your hands, with the shovels."

Most forty-niners panned for gold. They scooped soil into a pan and then swirled it with water. The trick was to wash away the lighter dirt so that only the heavier gold would remain, not an easy trick to master.

"Panning is to the beginner, a very curious and mysterious operation. Whirling and dipping with all my might . . . there was nothing in the appearance of the [dirt] to distinguish it from what I had seen a thousand times at home," noted one greenhorn, or new miner.

"Rocking" offered the chance to work faster. Working in teams, miners loaded dirt into a wooden box that resembled a baby's cradle. Miners washed the dirt and rocked the cradle, letting the watery mess run out an opening in the flat bottom. Cleats, or "riffles," attached to the bed caught the gold before it spilled out. Long boxes called Long Toms sluiced gold in the same fashion.

"Our feet are wet all day, while a hot sun shines down upon our heads, and the very air parches the skin like the hot air of an oven," one miner described the work. "After days of labor, exhausted and faint, we . . . [laid] down in our clothes—robbing our feet of their boots to make a pillow of them."

Diggings that failed to "pan out"—be rich in gold—were quickly abandoned. Reports of new finds set miners racing. Some miners spent their time "traveling about the country and prospecting, never satisfied with fair average diggings, but always having the idea that better were to be found elsewhere."

"Everyone was afraid he should be too late . . . that he should not find the fortune intended for him," said one forty-niner.

A few, like brothers John and Daniel Murphy, found treasure. Others discovered unending toil.

"I have now spent four months and one half in this place and worked hard and been diligent . . . and live . . . as I would hardly ask a dog to live," said Hiram Pierce, a blacksmith from New York.

"After all our preparations and hopes, our toil early and late, toil of the most laborious kind, digging, down in the . . . river till the water was up to our knees, giving ourselves barely time to eat, we have made but $4 each," another miner complained.

Worn down, one of every five forty-niners died from disease or accident within the first six months of arriving in California. One gold rusher believed that "when the suffering [of the miners] . . . is known, people will . . . be content to stay at home."

But people ignored the risks, harsh life, and long odds against hitting the jackpot, and kept coming. Perhaps they just felt "luckier." Whatever the explanation, by 1854, three hundred thousand had arrived in California making the gold rush one of the largest mass migrations in American history. Most were Yankees from New England and New York. One fourth were a hodgepodge mix of foreigners. Of these, the Chinese held the greatest number, about twenty-five thousand.

Beyond the common hardships faced by all the forty-niners, the foreigners encountered the added obstacles of anger and resentment. They were forced to pay a fee of twenty dollars a month when the state of California passed the Foreign Miners Tax in 1850. The additional expense drove thousands of them home.

Still, their fate paled beside that of the American Indians, who were expelled from the goldfields, killed by diseases carried by the forty-niners, enslaved, and murdered. Some goldfield towns even paid bounties for Indian heads and scalps. The California Indians' tragic fate is a national shame.

Among the hundreds of thousands of scruffy diggers, oppressed foreigners, and hunted American Indians, women were a tiny, tiny fraction. So rare were they that men would travel miles just to look at one. Hardworking women usually cooked and cleaned. One earned nine hundred dollars in nine weeks by taking in washing.

Luzena Wilson charged miners twenty-five dollars a week to be fed and found two hundred takers. She eventually built an inn, and even acted as the mining camp's "banker." Nancy Gooch came to the goldfields as a slave. There, her owner freed the black woman. She cooked and washed clothes for the miners. She toiled and saved her money, living a spare but independent life.

The women's experiences pointed to the real path to success in the gold rush: providing goods and services to the miners. As one miner explained, "Many are making great fortunes in a little time, but they do not make it by diggings. It is by trading and speculating."

Philip Armour walked six months from New York to California. But instead of panning for gold, he dug ditches. With his earnings, he opened a successful butcher shop. Levi Strauss joined the gold rush in 1850. He made sturdy pants with seams strengthened by copper rivets.

Strauss sold his clothes from his store in booming San Francisco. The city became something of the gold rush capitol as greenhorn forty-niners arrived at her port by the tens of thousands. About $345 million worth of gold from the diggings nearly two hundred miles away was taken to the city and banked . . . or spent. Restaurants and saloons sprang up and wild times followed.

SAN FRANCISCO

CALIFORNI

San Francisco's population multiplied to twenty-five thousand, sheltered in ramshackle buildings, tents, and even houses made of calico rags.

The initial gold fever of 1849 dampened after 1852. By the end of the decade, skilled engineers and heavy equipment replaced starry-eyed miners using pans and cradles.

And with it, ended the gold rush.

Did anyone get rich?

The Murphy brothers left the goldfields after just one year with an astounding $1.5 million. John Bidwell, a Sutter employee, unearthed a fortune and made himself one of California's finest citizens. A twelve-year-old boy worked $2,700 of gold from the ground in just two days.

But the great majority of forty-niners never found their fortune.

"I was no poorer than when I left," remarked Daniel Knower, the forty-niner who had endured the journey over the Isthmus. "I had acquired no wealth to astonish my friends with riches."

It was the merchants who profited the most from the great gold rush.

Armour transformed his meat business into a huge operation that still thrives. Strauss's hard-wearing and popular work pant "Levi's" became the great-great-granddaddy of modern blue jeans, spawning a fashion craze and an international industry. Goldfield grocery store owner Leland Stanford was able to become a great railway baron. Later, he was governor of California and established the renowned university bearing his name.

Leland Stanford

Yet the original characters from the start of the gold rush fared poorly.

John Sutter's dream of a personal empire was swept away as thousands of forty-niners made claims against the public lands he sought for himself. He resettled in Pennsylvania.

Loud-mouthed Sam Brannan, whose shouts of "Gold from the American River" triggered the gold rush, made a fortune and lost a fortune. He died penniless and forgotten in 1889.

John Sutter

John Marshall couldn't duplicate the luck that made him the first to discover gold. He never struck it rich. In fact, nothing in Marshall's life seemed to pan out, and he died broke and alone in 1885.

A man named Andrew Monroe buried him. Years earlier, Monroe had been a slave. His mother, a freed woman, toiled ten years to save enough money to purchase Monroe's freedom, as well as his wife's. The hardworking woman was cook and washerwoman of the diggings, Nancy Gooch.

The reunited family prospered and bought land. They even acquired a memorable piece on the banks of the American River: the site of Sutter's Mill.

Source Notes

First-hand accounts from the forty-niners themselves provided the base of my research for *Gold! Gold from the American River!* The best source for these was an online Library of Congress exhibit that included the full text and illustrations of 190 works documenting the California gold rush. All the quotes that I have included in *Gold!* were written by people who experienced the events themselves. The forty-niners whose stories I found most helpful were Samuel McNeil, Daniel Knower, Edward Washington McIlhany, and David Rohrer Leeper.

For descriptions of the times and conditions of California in 1849, I consulted several books by historians who have written about the gold rush. These books also frequently included quotes taken from accounts of forty-niners. In addition, I consulted Web sites that provided important statistics or dates. In all cases, I carefully selected and checked my sources for reliability.

California As I Saw It: First-Person Narratives of California's Early Years, 1849–1900. Library of Congress. http://lcweb2.loc.gov/ammem/cbhtml/cbhome.html.

Biographical Directory of the United States Congress: Bidwell, John, (1819-1900). http://bioguide.congress.gov/scripts/biodisplay.pl?index=B000447.

Groh, George. *Gold Fever.* New York: William Morrow & Company, 1966.

Infoplease. http://www.infoplease.com/ipa/A0110380.html.

Jackson, Donald Dale. *Gold Dust.* New York: Alfred A. Knopf, 1980.

Johnson, William Weber. *The Forty-Niners.* New York: Time-Life Books, 1974.

Kowalewski, Michael, ed. *Gold Rush: A Literary Exploration.* Berkeley, CA: Heyday Books, 1997.

Lewis, Oscar. *Sutter's Fort.* Englewood Cliffs, NJ: Prentice-Hall, 1966.

New Perspectives on the West. PBS. http://www.pbs.org/weta/thewest/program/episodes/three/daysof49.htm.

Oakland Museum of California. http://museumca.org/.

Paul, Rodman W. *The California Gold Discovery.* Gerogetown, CA: The Talisman Press, 1966.

Rosen, Fred. *Gold!* New York: Thunder Mouth Press, 2003.

Seidman, Laurence I. *The Fools of '49.* New York: Alfred A. Knopf, 1976.

Wallace, Robert. *The Miners.* New York: Time-Life Books, 1976.